Band-Aids, Bullet Holes and Bleeding Words

Carina Pellius

authorHOUSE®

AuthorHouse™ UK
1663 Liberty Drive
Bloomington, IN 47403 USA
www.authorhouse.co.uk
Phone: 0800.197.4150

Published by AuthorHouse 11/19/2015

ISBN: 978-1-5049-9432-3 (sc)
ISBN: 978-1-5049-9433-0 (hc)
ISBN: 978-1-5049-9434-7 (e)

Print information available on the last page.

Any people depicted in stock imagery provided by Thinkstock are models, and such images are being used for illustrative purposes only. Certain stock imagery © Thinkstock.

This book is printed on acid-free paper.

Because of the dynamic nature of the Internet, any web addresses or links contained in this book may have changed since publication and may no longer be valid. The views expressed in this work are solely those of the author and do not necessarily reflect the views of the publisher, and the publisher hereby disclaims any responsibility for them.

Band-Aids, Bullet Holes and Bleeding Words

Contents

This book is dedicated to those who have always encouraged me to write and perform my work.

Someday your pain will be useful
~ Ovid

Acknowledgements

First and foremost I want to thank God, he gave me the ability to be able to express myself through words, the gift of that outlet became my safe haven.

Next I would like to thank my mum, she doesn't know it, but she was the one who opened my eyes to poetry, before I was able to find my own words, I used to read hers and adapt them to become my own.

I also have to thank Louis Antwi, Michael Olabode and Ashley Joseph for pushing me as a young teenager to perform my work and put it out there, I was never brave enough to do it, but this book would never have come to life if you hadn't ever believed in me, motivated me and make me think my work was actually good.

This thanks then stems to Rachel Obiago and Iverson Chuks who actually managed to get me to perform two of the poems in this book, the reception I received afterwards was electrifying, that also gave me the motivation and belief to realise I could publish a book.

I would like to thank my loves and closest friends Malachi Bernard, Abim Anyiam and Peter Ikosa for helping me with the hard decisions of this book, without them this book most probably still wouldn't be published!

My first set of poems were topics given to me and my next set were from a real place, so lastly I would like to thank those who were the source of my emotions as well as those who inspired me to write these poems.

Introduction

Hi I'm Carina and it's really nice to meet ya.
I'm a little crazy but I assure you my brain cells are intact,
Blue tacked to make sure they stay where they need to be,
Processing all the information I see...you see, I'm a bit of a
nerd, science is my degree, so when I say someone is getting
on my nerves I mean the millions I have running through my
body,
Sorry,
I have so many parts to me, I thought it would just be easy to
tell you now, so I ought to show you my layers,

I use foundation on my face, it adds another layer to my
foundation so I can stand sturdy in public as I can be a bit
wobbly,
I use concealer to conceal my imperfections from this
imperfect world, I'm not sure if my nerves could take the pain
if I pealed back each layer to reveal my scars and bruises
you see,
Me, I'm a very outgoing person, I owe it to this mask, it shows
the permanent smile and spark in my eyes that I want you
to see.

But I have this other layer of skin, it's not so thick, quite unstable,
Umm...be careful of my self confidence stacked right there, it
seems high but it's stacked in a wobbly pile,
Oops, sorry
let me just move my insecurities off that chair, it's ok to stare, I
do, I haven't quite found a place to permanently put them yet.

So like I said I have a science degree, I'm quite proud of my millions of brain cells, but it's hard to change the image that my brain sells to me,
It's like my brain can hold me in a cell, stuck thinking the same things no matter how many times I try to talk myself out of it.

Take care of my words, they haven't formed properly, my lips stick together when I'm not wearing lipstick,
Sounds crazy I know but it makes it harder for my mouth to open and speak my mind without the confidence of that MAC lipstick called rebel,
It helps my lips to rebel against the force of my tongue that would rather sleep then be the strongest muscle it was meant to be, so when my words come out of my mouth, they sort of slip, slide and tumble out, so it can be hard to catch.

Hi my name's Carina and it's really nice to meet ya,
I like to write poetry when I have those days where I stare at the mirror and my words overwhelm me, oozing out of my tear ducts and nose because I know my lips are stuck,
My heart gathers the words lost and roaming and beats them into an orderly queue and pushes them out of my fingertips onto paper...1234...1234...
my heart starts to feel lighter, the words stand to attention in rows, forming sentences on the blank sheet,
A blank sheet I can use to wrap myself in and feel safe.
I let this sheet soak up all the weight of the heavy words I have been carrying, the weight drops off from my lips so a smile effortlessly emerges like a heavy object being released from a spring,
A spring in my step is what you see, and so I hope you take this time to really get to know me.

A note from the author:

A lot of people believe poets instantly have this amazing gift to write some of the most beautiful pieces ever written, but like any craft, you have to practice, you have to work on your craft and over time you can see your talent grow, and that's what we tend to show people, the growth, not so much the rough drafts or the poems that were born in the beginning, so before I show you my growth, I'd like to share a few from the beginning....
(Written between the years of 2000 and 2006)

What are the stars?

What are the stars?
The stars are like little silver coins

What are the stars?
The stars are bits of white paint flicked onto black paper

What are the stars?
The stars are little diamonds

What are the stars?
The stars are bright lamp posts far away

What are the stars?
The stars are big balls of gas hurling through space light
years away

What are the stars?
The stars are whatever you want them to be

School

The Teacher crams you up in a small classroom that seems
to last forever, minutes, hours, days, months, years.
The food smells nice but when they plop it onto your tray it
turns into mashed up bugs.
The teacher sometimes lets you breathe the outside world
and the noises get louder and louder until the dull life
regains its colours again.
Girls stand around the big black gates trying to get out,
but the bell goes and you know it's time to suffocate once
more.
As you slowly walk to class, the time stops so you can't miss
a second of learning,
It's school, school, SCHOOL!!!

Animals and plants

(This poem came in second place in a science poetry competition)

Plants that grow wild and free,
Contain cells like you and me.

Membranes, Nucleus, Cytoplasm,
Hard to say, but all plants have em.

Animals and plants may grow bigger,
But us humans have a better figure.

Animal's cytoplasm is the whole living matter,
Trying to remember all this in my brain is just a big clatter.

Animals and plants have wasted materials they have to excrete,
Ah that's better now, my poem is complete

Friendship

Friendship isn't something you can easily throw away,
Friendship isn't something you keep for just one day.
It is something that can last through your whole life time,
It's oh so very precious and it really isn't a crime.

Friendship is love, courageous and dependable,
Friendship is truth, honest and loyal.
Always keep it close to your heart,
Don't always stab at it like a board and a dart.

Friendship is something that takes time to grow,
It will be there forever and wherever you go.
Friendship takes tender love and care,
It is something that both you and your friends can share.

Bullies

Did you know when a chicken loses it head,
Runs the length of a football field,
Before it drops down dead?

It's like when a child has a bully,
And then the child runs and hides,
No time to prepare fully.

Not knowing what to do, they lose their head,
The bully knows what they are doing,
This is what they led.

The child tells, the bully pretends they're sweet,
The child is scared for what's coming,
It's time the bully beats.

The child is scared, they want to run away,
But there's nowhere to run and go,
They can't face another day.

The child has to think of their life ahead,
It's time to stop this right now,
The child drops down dead.

Time

Time is something to keep you on track,
It helps you organise your days,
There is a certain time for tears, laughter or to get a pat on
your back,
Time isn't always the same, it operates in different ways.

There is a time for thinking and a time for crying,
There is a time for feelings and a time for love,
There is a time for mourning when someone is dying,
Time helps God map out your life here and above.

Time puts everything into place,
Time has a future, present and past,
Time can let you know when to eat, sleep and have some
space,
Time can make you happy or sad and help the memories
last.

Abortion from the baby's eyes

Three months and the second week,
I wish I could come out and take a peek,
Now that I have begun to grow,
The world is a place I would like to know.

I wonder if my mummy loves me,
Her little girl I can't wait to be,
Because I love her too,
Our bond will be so strong and new.

Four months have gone past,
I can finally see some movement at last,
But terror is what I start to feel,
As a scary monster says "I'm coming to kill!"

I shout out "mummy please save me!"
I wonder if she can see what I see,
I become extremely scared,
As the scary monster neared.

I'm becoming weaker as he starts to tear me apart,
But the most pain I can feel is the breaking of my heart,
I want my mummy but cannot reach her,
My memories start to become a blur.

A beautiful light took me to a new place,
So though I cannot be your little girl in this time and place,
My life I have now started anew,
But I just wanted you to know, I'll always love you.

Just Remember

If you ever need a caring friend,
Just remember I'm always around,
I'll help you now and forever, until the bitter end,
I'll even be your cushion when you fall to the ground.

People may not understand what you're going through,
Which makes you more depressed and sad,
You have no idea how to cope or what to do,
Your best friend's not even there so you feel mad.

But as life struggles on and things seem to get worse,
And all you want is someone's shoulder to cry on,
Just remember I'm here and will always turn up first,
I may not be your best friend but I'll never be gone.

When you need advice or just an ear,
Don't ever be afraid to call or ask,
Because when you call I'll be right there,
You'll never meet someone who could move so fast.

But life will get better, it's not always so hard,
Just remember I'm your friend, and if you need it I'll give you
that space,
I'll do my best to take away what's mentally scarred,
Because just remember my friendship to you, no one can
erase.

Never forget

They say *'from broken wings*
To falling stars,
God mad everything,
But unbreakable hearts'.

So when you feel alone,
And there's no one out there to love,
Just remember you're beautiful inside,
And there's someone that loves you up above.

So I hope you know if dreams came true,
Someone would surely want to be here with you,
They say *'don't think to the world you're one person,*
but to one person you mean the world'.

So God in heaven, yes God above,
Please protect my friend I love,
Sent with a smile and sealed with a kiss,
Never forget someone loves the person who just read this.

Love

Love can be felt with more than one emotion,
Oh how we'd try to get it by taking a potion.

Love is not always easy to express,
It has consequences that either turn out bad or a success.

Love is not an easy thing to understand,
It has its own timing, it doesn't come at your command.

Love is what completes the hole in your heart,
Without it your world seems like it'll fall apart.

Everyone wants to be loved and have that feeling,
When your heart feels broken it can be quite healing.

There are different ways to feel love, it can mean many things,
It makes you feel happy, special, or the ability to fly with
wings.

Love can be a feeling for someone special, your family or a
friend,
If you feel that no one loves you remember someone does,
If you don't find them in this world, then I pray you will up
above.

Thirteen

As she stared into the mirror she slit her wrist,
She held in the pain and clenched her fist,
She closed her eyes tight as she saw her life go by,
Her painful memories flashed up as she cried "why
oh why?"

She pressed hard with a cloth to stop the blood from
flowing,
Then stretched her sleeve to stop the cuts from showing,
She dried her eyes, took a deep breath and walked out the
bathroom,
Then locked herself in her bedroom, to hide herself from the
gloom.

The next day she got dressed and headed for school,
She applied her lipstick and mascara to make herself look
cool,
The wrong crowd introduced her to sex and drugs,
She snuck out to parties and had sex with thugs.

She'd stare out the window and watch people in their cars,
And close her eyes and wish she could go somewhere far,
Her mum's partner hits her, her mum pretends she
doesn't see,
Then she'd look deep within herself and again question
"why me?"

Outside she acts tough like she is unstoppable,
But when she's inside a good life is impossible,
Tossing and turning at night, her past haunts her,
And when she awakes, her good times are a blur.

Her friends give her LSD to make her feel high,
So she'll forget her troubles and feel as if she can fly,
She thinks only drugs and alcohol can make her smile,
Because without it at home grins come to her once in a
while.

Deep blue eyes, black eyelashes, red lips and a pale face,
Don't bother staring too hard, her feelings left without a
trace,
Slit wrists, lungs full of smoke and a bag full of cocaine,
Her friends changed her and now she's consumed with all
her pain.

Abuse

Just got married and so in love,
My husband and I just can't get enough.
All I wanted was a man to love me,
And this was the guy who wanted it to be.

I remember in secondary school where we first met,
The moment our eyes joined that's when my heart set.
But he was taken and sadly so was I,
So we used to watch each other while life passed by.

But one day when I was alone in the park,
The love of my life sat next to me in the dark.
We spoke for hours and in love we did fall,
I was so happy and smiling that I finally had it all.

But years after marriage he began to drink,
And now he hits and beats me, he just doesn't think.
But I can't leave him we've been through so much together,
On our wedding day I cried as he said his love is forever.

But as I sit here in silence I can hear the engine of the car,
My husband had just got back from yet another bar.
He walked in swearing, looked at me and slammed the
door,
Then he came and slapped me and I hurled to the floor.

I cried and said I loved him so much with all my heart,
He stopped and smiled at me then called me a worthless tart.
He said I was useless, hit me and spat in my face,
Every day I endure this pain; I don't know how much more I
can take.

His face turned wicked, his brown eyes so cold,
I couldn't escape, nowhere to run, I just had to be bold.
He bent down to my level, held my neck and spoke,
He yelled 'answer me woman!', I couldn't and I started to choke.

He held my neck tighter and pursed my lips,
His eyes met mine and I saw flames lit.
He kicked me and punched me and told me to die,
I lay on the floor whimpering, trying not to cry.

My lip bust, face swollen and my hips were bruised,
My leg bled, why didn't I leave when I was first abused?
So many women are in my place and also feel my pain,
Some of us leave but some come back because we love them again and again.

I managed to get up, looked to the door making a quick dash,
But as weak as I was, I was slow; he caught me in a flash.
He threw me against the wall and said I was the cause of his trouble,
He cried as I leaned against the wall in a huddle.

He kissed my cheek, I thought it was over and reached for the door,
But it wasn't, he wasn't done and told me he didn't love me anymore.
He grabbed for a knife, I knew this was the last breath I would take,
Not only was my body in pain but I had a terrible heartache.

He held me close, stabbed me and left me to drop to the floor,
I looked at him; he looked down as he watched the warm blood pour.
I gasped for air as he left me to die and I watched the room spin,
I was dying a slow painful death like a bullet pierced deep within.

He used to be so kind, so lovely and so free,
I just don't know how I didn't foretell the man he came
to be.
Everyone loved him, not an enemy in his life,
I thought I was the luckiest girl to be made his wife.

Now I'm gone I want you to know you have a right not to be
a victim,
When you first see the signs get out while you can so you
don't feel the pain deep within.

Euthanasia

Staring as the sunlight glistens on the deadly cup,
Waiting for the right moment to say I've had enough,
My breath is slow, but my heart beats fast,
Just waiting for this nervous feeling to pass.

Lying in my new home, dwelling on my pain,
Family and friends crying that life won't be the same,
No words can pass my lips, no expressions on my face,
Nothing is what I feel, bitterness is what I taste.

Watching the outside world as they move and grow,
looking in my water's mirror, my painful tears flow,
My daughter's stood over me, hugging me so tight,
I snuggled in deeply knowing I couldn't last the night.

She looked down at me, her tears mixed with mine,
As I looked at her face, pain caught up with time,
I looked back at the cup that would save me,
Filled to the brim in sleeping pills that will let it be.

I held my daughter's hand and directed her to the cup,
She followed my watery eyes and gasped as she looked up,
I tried to smile, she knew everything would be alright,
I squeezed her hand so she knew I could no longer fight.

She looked at me, I saw my reflection in her eyes,
I knew she didn't want to, these things she did despise,
I rested her hand on my heart so she knew I would always
love her,
But pain I couldn't react to was making life a blur.

As she brought the cup over, a tear ran down her cheek,
I wanted to reassure her, but words I could not speak,
I looked at my reflection through her tears, but all I saw was pain,
We both knew it was illegal, such a risky game.

I was filled with pain that I knew she could see,
This risky thing was the only way to set me free,
This was the only way I could live again,
Lord I pray for my grieving daughter, amen.

I let her know that I'd always be a part of her,
We both know that cancer has no cure,
I knew she wondered how I felt, but she'd never know,
I always felt like I was left in this cold alone.

I tried to pretend I lived in a fantasy,
But it could never have meaning, it was just only me,
One by one the pills slipped down,
Little by little my daughter's face grew a frown.

I made her take my precious locket,
Which held our picture, she put it in her pocket,
We hugged and kissed one last time.
Time of death...half past nine.

Ghetto

Police report on the news that yet another black boy is
dead,
His parents are filled with anger and sorrow.
I walk down the streets with my hands in my pocket,
Observing the torn down building and the work of art on
the walls.

Little boys playing basketball using a shopping trolley as
their net,
Teenage girls with their skirts so high pushing babies along
the road,
Grown men with their heads down rolling weed at the
corner of the street,
Do they really believe life is meant to be this way?

Always witnessing crimes or being involved,
Always going to bed knowing that rich red blood will stain
their hands,
Always running from the police with a boot full of dirty
money,
Always crying on your bed alone holding your stomach and
knowing.

Everyone ducks with their hands over their ears screaming
with terror,
People running and shooting, lives being lost, blood being
poured.
People who don't know about the ghetto try to act like
they are,
People who don't know about the ghetto act proud to be
there.

But people who live in the ghetto don't want to act like it,
People who live in the ghetto are not proud to be where
they are.
Some have pity on the young people who want to be from
the ghetto,
They have pity because they know these youngsters could
never survive it.

When you get called ghetto, people brush it off,
They take it as a joke, and use the same line themselves,
But if you lived in the ghetto, worked in the ghetto and died
in the ghetto,
Would you really be telling yourself it's cool to live in the
ghetto?

Adopted

When I woke up this morning, I stared across my room,
I stared at where my little brother sleeps,
He always seems so happy and calm,
I can't say the same for me.

I put on a t-shirt and made my way to the kitchen,
Everyone was already in there having breakfast,
My little brother and sister fighting over the toy from the cereal box,
Mum in her dressing gown by the sink sipping tea,
Dad adjusting his tie with a biscuit in his mouth.

This family look so cosy even though their actions don't show it,
They all have a feature that connects them,
May it be their nose, eyes or feet, they're connected,
Then you have me, leaning on the kitchen door,
So far yet so close, not a feature could match theirs.

Later when I watched my little sister flick through baby pictures,
She smiled with memories filling her innocent eyes,
Something I could never do,
It's as if my childhood had been erased so I only reminisce on what I see now.

I often thought about how I looked or acted as a baby,
What my first word was, or who saw my first step,
To other people it's no big deal, but to me it is,
As hard as I close my eyes, clench my fists and purse my lips,
All I can remember from my babyhood was 'CRASH!'

It doesn't matter what I do or they say, I could never really fit in,
To them I'm their eldest son and older brother, but to the outside world...
I'm adopted...

Note from the author:

That was the start, here is my present, these next set of poems are when I really started to find my writing style, when I started to write only when I was inspired, rather than just given a topic...

Still I love you

As a scientist I know my whole body is filled with nerves,
And you somehow manage to get on every single one of
them.
Have me struggle to keep the tears in by counting from one
to ten,
Have me arguing and fuming for hours on end,
And then,
Still have me wishing I could just be with my boo,
Wanting you so near so that I can just embrace you,
Have me wondering if at any time you've felt the same
way too.

Sometimes midway in fights I would think why
Do we battle back and forth?
Why are you not the guy
Who just apologises and shows affection,
To show me we have a connection,
Instead of fighting about each feeling I mention?

You could make me burst into tears,
Infected with fears,
Thinking after being together for more than a year,
The love and relationship would slowly disappear,
Because to me it was never really clear,
If you loved me as much as I do you.
Because during them fights,
Trying to see who was right,
You would always break out with wise cracks
To wind me up that I would then verbally attack,
Because while you were wisely cracking
And affection lacking,
I was the one who felt so low,

But was still willing to go,
That extra mile just to take fault and apologise,
To help dry the pain from my red eyes,
And for you to realise,
How much I despised,
This game,
Of who's to blame,
Because you never acted the same.

Then I am reminded of how much I love you,
From the verbal attacks to the wise cracks reminds me,
Opposites attract.

We fit together like Ying and Yang,
A piece of both of us in both of us,
To show even though we're different and can be opposite,
We attract,
Even during fights I think well that romantic crap
Didn't last,
Funny how it's said and soon enough,
The happiness dies fast.
But you compliment me,
Like the air I breathe,
Lying with you and stroking your hair and face sooths me,
And I cannot object,
That we connect.

I hate those times you say 'don't do it'
But I push that little further just to see your reaction,
Hoping that it's nothing and I'm left with the satisfaction,
Of doing it anyway, rebelling against the forceful words you
told me,
But in exchange you make me see,
A look that was specially made for me,
As you turn your body and say 'fine carry on',
Knowing that it will make me stop and feel sorry,
Damn your reverse psychology.

Yet still I cannot deny,
Even when I have to cry,
You're there to comfort me and love me,
And make me feel that I'm safe and everything will be fine,
That is why I love you.

What's fi dinna?

Madda madda wha fi dinna?

Dat chicken you a play wid in de garden once we skin her

Madda madda you cyaan do dat!
Is dat why yuh giving her de special food, fi mek her fat?

Where you tink de goats an de pigs go an all dem
sinting der?
That curry mutton n salsa had u go fi seconds me swear
Me never did see such a big mout
So gwan wid urself before me clap off dat pout

Madda madda what will papa seh?

Hush now child yuh fadda nah buy dem fi steh
Meat haf fi come from somewhere, dey nah grow pon trees
They nah like de ackee or banana or me famous rice an peas
Tap de noise an lef me nah, kiss me neck back
Stop twis up yuh mout an go tek off de sunday suit
Before de breeze blow weh dah hat
Wipe yuh nose an dats de end of dat

Me nah wan chicken fi dinna, me tek her away so
Me ah hide her like a tief in de night an yuh will never know
Yuh nah bodda her no, yuh nah budda her no more
Me tek her to a foreign lan, where she will live fi sure

Hmm mek sure yuh fill up yuh purse wid money,
But nah tell me nuttink wen yuh belly fi seh it hungry
Gwaan find a foreign lan, gwan please do
Mek sure if yuh come back yuh got fi somewhere to come
back to!

The best feeling in the world

The stars twinkled sympathetically as they shone trying to make me glow,
The moon looked down sharing its artificial heat with me,
As if it tried to comfort me with a warm 'I'm-here-for-you' hug.

The sky was a dark deep blue acting as an ocean of sorrow,
As it worked with the wind trying to wash the pain away,
But here I sit alone,
In the middle of my new found pain,
Wiping away the salty tears that wickedly burn my eyes,
And hugging a loving teddy trying to escape the piercing feeling of my heart hurting.

I look down cowardly into a puddle the sky had made not so long ago,
As if it were crying not only with me but for me,
Scared of seeing the image the clear water would make,
I saw a girl who was so bruised she struggled to look back
The big smile she once wore had been ripped away,
Her tears trying to build a brick wall slowly hiding the emotion,
But failing,
She clung to her top trying to hide her bruised and abused heart.

I looked into the teary sky and made a simple wish:
Twinkle twinkle little star,
Tell me why you are so far,
Can't you heal my breaking heart?
Hold me close so pain will part.
Twinkle twinkle little star,
Why can't I be where you are?

Why do people have to feel such pain?
Why does it dig so deep?
Nothing can stop it ruling your heart and demanding its
place as if it were king,
You think once your heart defeats it,
The pain will not dig so deep next time around,
But I was wrong,
To this pain I was merely a child and it found great pleasure
in trying to rob me of my innocence and it cruelly smiled as
it saw how naïve I had once been.

Even though the heart may win the battle,
It does not win the war,
The pain is so fiery, stubborn and determined,
It will fight again,
With the same amount of pain,
In the same depth,
If not more.

It's one war that can never be won,
As it is constantly fought till your dying days,
It's as if God and Lucifer are fighting within your very soul,
God as the heart trying to restore faith, serenity and
strength,
While Lucifer plots to make the heart burn and feel pain it
has never felt before,
Inflicting doubt, anxiety and tiredness,
The very thing that is the best feeling in the world can hurt
uncontrollably...it is love...

Procrastination

"Look at me" I can hear him whispering, "let's find something else to do,
You're thinking too hard put the books down, let's find the fun side of you!"
'My heart is willing but my flesh is weak' I say to myself as I force myself to carry on typing,
"Come on, let's catch up on a program" he whispers, "how about Skyping?"
I chew on my pen lid and I try to block out his poisonous words,
But I cannot deny how charming he is, as he points out the singing birds.
"We can stop working for just an hour" he whispers, I am seduced by his power,
But I know in the back of my head if I stop now it will be hours past that one hour.

'I do need to catch up on Cougar Town' I say to myself in my head,
But he can read my face like a book and makes me clear some space on my bed,
"Get comfortable!" he says, "lie down, I think we were on episode three",
"Who knows, maybe there's more out now, we can watch them all, let's see!"
My will power is starting to break and my motivation is running low,
"I need to get this work finished" I say, but he's already directing my eyes to watch the show.

I bit my lip as I feel myself slowly submitting to him,
He flashes that award winning smile and closes the book I'm trying to skim,

"I want you to be my queen" he softly whispers in my ear,
I feel myself crack a smile but this is my deepest fear,
"Queen?" I repeat, "queen" he smiles back,
What else has he got up his sleeve to steer me off track?

"I've had a month to do this work, it's due in three days time!"
"You should be enjoying yourself" he says, "after all, you are
in your prime",
I tell myself that I still have time left, watching a show won't
hurt,
But these are the thoughts he's planted in me, he's always
so alert,
I keep a smile on my face but I'm not fooling anyone
but me,
I'll be the one to suffer if I don't hand in this work done
properly.

Tears are not a sign of weakness but a show of strength,
For they can trickle down your skin and expose your very heart
in a way words could never do.

I want

I want to be the Ice Queen with a cold heart of stone,
I want to leave the life of a peasant and sit upon my throne.
I want to stop the warm blood from pumping to feel the
ease,
So that I'm no longer struggling or trying hard to breathe.

I never needed a knight; I used to save myself,
I used to be my own king, never needed anyone else's
wealth.
I just want to take all these feelings and place them back in
Pandora's box,
I should have known better than to open it and now I can't
find the lock.

I want to pull out the feelings like a clown would pull on rope,
I would pull and pull and pull until I wasn't so full of hope.
I am drowning in the hurt that I lived through to glimpse
those single days of good,
Only hope could do that, now I wish it never could.

I want to look at your face and not be sucked in by your ways,
Because at the end of it all it's my heart that has to pay.

Who do you see?

You look in the mirror and who do you see?
The beautiful tanned lady with straight hair and long legs...
that image you saw on T.V.?
The girl with luscious lips and sparkling eyes that sways her
hips until every sperm carrying male is hypnotised?

You look at your reflection in a puddle and who do you see?
The girl with the wet hair but yet shows sex appeal so that
her sex appeals?
The image of the raindrops magnifying every curve or bump
that makes a girl look hot,
The image that guys chase after because your beauty can
be destroyed with just one spot.

You flick through the adverts on T.V. and who do you see?
You see every girl with everything that's perfect while you
watch in awe and say "why not me?"
You become exposed to these subconscious demands to
do something to your hair so that you can get a man to
come over here,
Because the way your hair is, just isn't acceptable...well
that's what the T.V. said right?
So you're forced to fight, making your bum tight and your
weight light to look like a model,
Because the T.V. criticises you if you waddle or your skin isn't
flawless, and that you should be ashamed if you can't walk
around topless, because the T.V. says you're too curvy, so
you feel unworthy to step out into the finger pointing world.

When you look in shop windows who do you see?
Girls hidden behind products, that with their different
features, they can become a new person.

So like a spell you become enchanted applying everything
just so you can have a chance...at being beautiful,
because the T.V. teaches you to not be natural on a
subconscious level, so you're sucked in by this devil that tells
you the way you were born isn't the norm and what you
wear isn't how it's worn, so that you become worn out by
constantly fighting.

Make up doesn't change you, if anything it can enhance
your features, it definitely
just decorates it, but then people congratulate it and this
stimulates your desire for more.
The media says this is what you want, and if you want men,
this is what they like so this is what you need, so they plant
this seed and your taken over by greed piling draws and
shelves high until you can't even see half the things you
have, because without it you're not beautiful enough, you
don't want your hair to be tough or your skin too rough
because then you won't be beautiful...enough! Yes you can
enhance your lips and sway your hips and dye your hair,
pick the sexiest clothes to wear.

But when you look in the mirror who do you see?
I don't see the girl on T.V. telling me my hair isn't straight
enough, or if it's straight my hair is lifeless, or if it's poufy it's a
terrible afro, am I supposed to live my life less?
I don't see the model who walks the runway, tall and thin
with no hips
I don't see the girl with the greatest lipsticks to enhance my lips
If I completely change my hair, decorate my face, and slim
down who am I trying to be?...not me.

When I look in the mirror who do I see?
No billboard, T.V. magazine girls, I see me
I see the girl who isn't perfect but that's who I want to be,
I see a girl who yes wears extensions or weaves, who
decorates her face, who shaped her eyebrows...but not so

a guy would see me and raise his eyebrows...ok so it may be a little for them but it has to always be mainly for me.

I see a girl with big brown eyes, a funny nose and who is tall but not thin and still wears a grin, a girl who is curvy but I don't feel unworthy, I see the girl who's imperfections and rough edges give her edge, who's curvy body gives her a different body to everybody.

We are given opinions on how we should look...so I look, and I look...and I look like me, and sometimes I frown but most times I like what I see, and I'm not trying to be anything that I'm not, and if some boys don't think I'm hot, then maybe to them I'm not,
But I don't care, plenty more fish in the sea who will open their eyes wide enough to see...just me, not somebody made up by the T.V. and if the media wants to look down on me, then I'll just look up you'll see,
Love who you are, not what the media says you should love, you can't make yourself look pretty if you hate yourself on the inside, because inside is where the true beauty lies... right?

Fragments of Love

My heart is filled with blood, pumping it around every aspect of my body, and along with it, fragments of love,
That ride along the tides of my blood and pricks parts of me like fragments of glass,
when I hold your hand, I feel the pricks of the love like glass, sending Chinese whispers to my synaptic nerves, which you climb aboard and stand on top of like a king and I walk away with the fragments of love pricking my face to make it crumble and it looks like I'm mad at you,
You filled my blood with fragments of love that combine and collide into each other causing pain that only you can cure, the tender feeling of your lips that part ever so slightly like the red sea and send a pain relief that shoots through my body, giving me a burst of an artificial high, that slowly settles and disappears as if it was never there, and like an addict I crave it, I walk, feeling every prick in my toes, fingers, muscle movements because my muscles are like elephants, with a memory sharper than my own, tearing and breaking me down, to heal and grow back stronger,
But I always feel weak, anaemic, I can't blame you, saying that you've robbed me of my oxygen, that you've taken my breath away, because I handed it over freely, replaced the oxygen with your fragments of love, which they say conquers all things, It's truly conquered me, tied me down with the strings in my heart and made me surrender.
I trick myself, to pretend there is no heart in my chest, there are no fragments of love flowing through my body, but you make me open up my body to you, pull out my beating heart and wear it on my sleeve so that you can admire it like art when you want to, and I am left like a juggler trying to juggle everyday chores while trying not to drop my heart, and I come to you when you call, because I can't escape the beautiful music

you play when you pluck the strings embedded in my heart, and you give me a look, that you hand over as a gift once in a blue moon, that sends sparks in my body and makes my heart beat faster so that you can get a higher note on my strings.

I need to pee

I need to pee,
To breathe and feel at ease,
To sit on the toilet seat,
Staring down at my crossed feet,
And let the feeling flow through me,
Like the air that I breathe,
And the pee that I pee.

I need to pee,
To sit comfortably upon that toilet seat,
Close my eyes and let my troubles flee.
Just unhooking the button in my jeans,
And feeling the release of tightness overwhelm me.

I need to pee,
Jumping up and down to see,
If I can hold it in me,
Just until I get to the toilet seat,
No one in the bathroom except me (maybe my cat too),
Sighing with relief and thinking about,
my daily goings that surround me.

I am about to pee,
About to feel the rush of anxiety,
Leave me and be filled with comfortability.

I'm going to pee,
As the pee enters the toilet,
I feel so free I just have to sigh with relief,

Especially when you have held it in as long as me,
I lay back on the toilet seat, smiling with my eyes closed
because...
I finally got to pee.

Touch

He lay her down as if to put her to sleep,
Keeping close to preserve body heat, that would soon expand.
He tried to satisfy her deepest desires as did she,
He rubbed her body with oil which had a warming sensation and would make her skin smooth and silky,
Silky enough so that when she gently rubbed his pride and massaged his ego, he would be able to pass through her gates of passion with ease.
They move as one,
Body intertwined,
Heat building up and covering the room like a warm blanket,
They make sounds that could be described as lovers music.
She moved down letting her tongue explore,
Looking for the place where pleasure lives,
As her tongue dances down happily, it comes across a place where her partner held the key to the gates of her feminine cave.
Explored by him many times as he leaves fireworks on her sexual grounds.
The passion grew like wild flowers in summer,
And the lovers song became louder so that you could feel the intensity with every note.
The smell of each other's perfume lifted from their bodies and into the ruffled bed sheets.
This time he let his tongue out of the teeth cage,
So it could do its own exploring.
As his tongue happily made its way around every bump and curve looking for a place magical enough to explore,
He came across kissable lips that also acted as gates to his partner's forbidden sanctuary.

His tongue stood firm as it opened the gates and marched up and down leaving its wet trail behind as if to show it's marking the area.
After the fireworks had been let off and the gates of passion were closed for the night,
The bodies retreated to their resting place before opening time returned.

Some people say long distance relationships don't work,
But look at the sun and the moon,
They spend their days and nights apart,
And in those precious moments where they finally come together,
Their love covers the sky.

Identity

"Who are you?" Said a screwed up face,
"Dressing like them, talking like them, find your own place in society!
Because no one said there were rules in how you should look,
If you stopped for a second to learn a lesson about the way you were dressing,
You would realise all the answers are in something you don't read often,
A book!
You would see that people in prison had their belts taken away from them so they couldn't hang themselves,
But you have a lot more sense and wealth and should have enough respect for yourself instead of copying everyone else.
God gave you your own body, your own face, your own mind,
So that you could be a spectacular individual, one of a kind.
But you feel the need to plead, taken over by greed just to feed your mind with information like,
That in order to be somebody you have to copy somebody,
Wearing 'phat' chains, high heeled shoes or baggy tracksuits like the celebrities on TV,
Who send subliminal messages saying "be like me!", why can't you just be you?
Dress a little different, have something decent to say, be who you are then you'll be somebody instead of copying somebody because you weren't born with anybody and if you were, even that body is different to yours...right?
If we were all supposed to be the same don't you think we would be?
Don't be so naive thinking everything you see is true on TV
Do you think killing people makes you 'bad' because your so called gang said so?

Why would you sink so low to get people to know the identity you crave for,
And it isn't even yours?
Is that what you want to show?
A fabricated truth,
Have your own identity, you don't need to be like anybody other than the one body you're in.
Because your own personality helps make up your identity, then you'll be somebody,
Because you're different",
Said the screwed up face as angry tears fled down their cheek.
I couldn't mistake that face, the time or the place,
Because that face told me these things out of affection, protection and not to mention a lesson,
Because it was my own mind,
Yes, my reflection.

Dear Uterus

Dear Uterus,

We need to talk....

It's not me, it really is you,

For some reason, you have let society make you think we have to be at war with one another, but you are a part of me, therefore we really should be one, I don't even know how many times I have to sing the Lion King song (We are One) to you for you to really understand that.

I get that Eve ate the apple and so you feel it's your destiny to inflict pain on me, but you're missing two key facts

1) That was the old testament, God in the new testament would be like, "yo uterus, my son has come to Earth, I understand humans more now, chill"

2) My parents had me baptised as a baby, which is supposed to wash away that sin so that I am pure...which means you're pure and you no longer have to carry Eve's burden anymore

So based on that, I have no idea why you're trying to kill me from the inside,

Aren't you tired?

I knowwww you must be dying for a baby and you see all these girls out there with theirs and you're wondering "where the heck is mine?!?!?"

But listen uterus, patience is a virtue, body clock, heart and brain all understand that and they have no desire for me to have babies now, so with that said, you need to be a big uterus AND GROW THE HELL UP!!!!! Because I am literally sick and tired of your temper tantrums every damn month, 12 YEARS!!!! (...I calculated it) I've had to put up with this and I'm sooooooo done, you need to stop throwing lightening, kicking, pinching, stabbing and whatever else you do inside me and just be easy like Sunday morning (like the song),

I promise I will give you a baby, just wait around 4/5 years, you've waited 25, so 4/5 years isn't even a thing.
But the hot flushes, cold flushes, pain, stabbing pain, cramps, stitches, heavy flows, increased tiredness, lack of sleep and decreased appetite has to stop, because no one else in my household is dealing with it, so really why should I?

You're making me wish for menopause or to have you removed, both I agree are very premature thought processes, but you're turning me into a crazy person who tries to take naps under her desk at work, we can't keep on with this world war, we need to be united, we need to be one body, in sync instead of both running and crying to mother nature.

Yours lovingly
Me (because obviously you know who I am)

Paper war

She writes her feelings down on paper, trying to make these words escape her
Fighting for the ink to make some sort of print as she scribbles to exemplify herself from her emotions that notion this wave of passionate feelings, that has her racing and chasing to catch her breath, to catch herself, to calm her nerves.

But the ink doesn't create even the smallest of words, it starts to form a letter but disappears as she finishes. How can she show people how she's feeling, if she can't even find the letters to make words, to make some sense and reclaim some strength that she had childishly left behind, so now she finds herself stabbing at this piece of perfect white paper, trying to destroy its claim of serenity and peace, making it as weak as she feels by bombarding it with tears that she knows will dampen it and eventually create holes, because if she cannot express herself with ink, then she will express it with visual sensations, for actions speak louder than words, these dents in the paper speak up, while the tears shout out in pain...her pain.

She feels a smile crack through the stiffness, finally beginning to feel sane, knowing she can take out her frustration and reclaim herself.
She finds herself out of her jurisdiction, struggling to move while she feels this restriction on her heart, if it gets any heavier it's sure to break, she holds her chest, she doesn't know how much more of this she can take, she leans back, trying to take deep breaths, trying to regain composure knowing closure is what she needs to think freely again, to feel at ease.

You have my heart breaking out of my chest,
My breath trailing behind, feeling the relief of stress,
Love doesn't always keep you in your right mind

Trapped

I have so many words, feelings and emotions locked up in my head,
I've thought about speaking but there's too many unsaid.
I've created a brick wall to hide behind and stay quiet,
There have been times I thought I was brave enough to speak,
But when I open my mouth,
I stop,
And stay silent.
When I'm asked "how are you?" I'm just about to speak the truth,
But instead say what you want to hear,
Because you only want a simple answer,
Could you handle me if I came clear?
I'm trapped by these cursed words that I feel,
Scared to come clean so I'm trapped behind these bars of steel,
They trap my mind not allowing the thoughts to be free.
So while I'm crying,
And dying,
Inside, a smile is what I let you see.
I'm a prisoner,
A prisoner of the worst kind, I'm a prisoner of
Myself.
My head feels like, to it I'm holding a hard steel gun,
Because I'm scared and a prisoner so there's nowhere to run,
And all of this is happening to me all because,
I'm holding my tongue.
You might say "just speak what you feel, and then you can be free",
But if you look deep into my soul and mind you'll know it's not that easy,

Do you think I like it? Being trapped inside myself and no one can see?
I could be destined to stay like this my whole life…eternity.
I listen to all your problems envious of how free you seem,
But for me to speak up and sing my sorrow is only a wishful dream.
So here I sit,
A prisoner of thoughts and feeling unsaid,
With lonely meaningful words trapped in my head,
Haunting me while I'm wrapped up in bed.
But when I can't take it anymore and can't stand to be quiet,
I stand up and open my mouth and look around,
But I stop,
And stay silent.
I slowly sit down and pick up my headache gun,
Wishing to get rid of these words held by my tongue,
Remembering I'm a prisoner of the worst kind,
I'm a prisoner of myself.

I am

I am the clown who owns the centre stage, pulling faces, making jokes and wanting to be the one who makes an excellent choice of being someone's company,

I am the magician who somehow puts a smile on frowned faces, doing or saying random things that no one expects but expects,

I am the psychiatrist listening to problems, empathising, sympathising, handing out the best advice I believe is right, trying my hardest to make their troubles melt away,

I am the solider first in line standing to attention to take the blows given rightfully or wrongfully to protect the team called family

I am the worker, making sure deadlines are met, whether they are for a university degree, a business or household chores

I am the restless child, seeking attention and adventure, curious as to what's around the corner

I am the minute hand on a clock, trying to push it faster than a second, wanting time to get a move on so I can see what will happen in an hour, today, next week or a few years from now

I am the actress, so poised at receiving yet another award for best actress in the films by pretending to be happy when life is crumbling around you, but you have to make sure you're strong...or at least act it, because that is what you won the award for.

You pluck at my heart strings and strum a tune that only I can hear,
And the music is so passionate that I can feel it deep within me,
And in those moments I pray that you forever only play this
song for me.

Dearest Heartbeat

To my dearest heartbeat,
Thank you for keeping me alive and for being healthy to allow me to conquer things in the world.
Thank you for keeping up with me when I'm on the go, for not holding me back and saying "you can't", but beating faster and saying "don't stop".
When I need clarity and time to think, you give me something to focus on, allowing me to keep my thoughts in time with your rhythm,
You never leave me, you keep me in tune and in time...123, 123, 123...

Thank you for agreeing with me when I see things in life that I feel are breathtaking, because only you skip a beat to let me know you're just as excited or in awe as I am, you help me realise the beauty in the world that others may not share with me.
You always let me know you're there when silence consumes the world around me and I start to feel alone.

No one could have a better companion in life than you,
Until death do us part my beating heart.

Forever yours
Me

Sister

Sister how do I love thee? Let me count thy ways,
You snuck up on mum and battled your way through her womb,
You should have been a race car driver, it's tiring watching you zoom,
Through life, hobbies, styles and friends,
You know just how to drive me right around the bend,
memorising my friend's phone numbers, copying my hand writing, drawings, actions
and then...wait....where was I going with this?

When we were young, you tried so hard to be like me and outshine me,
trying to be as close in age as possible, picking your birthday two months ahead of mine, but picking the second day of the month just like mine, I bet it was to spite me.

Now you're nothing like me, being the lightening to my clear nights,
where did you get all that thunder?
The only time you're peaceful is in your slumber.

You're like this puzzle with so many more pieces than me to assemble, but because you were so sneaky and eager to arrive, mum and dad didn't get the manual,
They've been trying so hard to get you on the right path, they handed you a compass and pointed out the north star, but you hardly stayed on track, though I guess some people would admire that, it keeps them on their toes, not the part of you that hides all your woes and building foes out of mum, dad, me and the other three.

It's a mission trying to pin your shadow to you and stop you using off all the fairy dust to fly around like a bird through life and temptations.

You were never meant to wear my shadow, you were always trying to run ahead, through life you have sped and it surprises me that you're not even tired yet.

So I am the one who falls into your shadow, while you run ahead, instead of growing ahead with need, growth and spirit...wait, is that my t-shirt?
Still not wanting to be like me but using my clothes to make some kind of identity, as if to say I am the rough draft and you could make a better version of me.

There's so much I could teach you if you would just listen, but then there'd be so much more you could tell me and say that I don't understand you, so you bury your feelings in the sand but at the same time you try to stand so much taller than me.

You are Ying and I am Yang, we are no longer the two little dickey birds who had sung the high pitched songs of youthfulness and kiddie games.

But you know it's cool, some tigers weren't meant to be tame, so I'll watch you zoom little sister through the things you do,
While I struggle to remember the tame you,
I guess I have a spot that loves you, let me count thy ways...

Grey matter

When the big indistinguishable shades of grey rise through the gaps of the black and white, you let it consume you, you let it take away your breath and your words, you let the grey fog your clarity, your ability to decipher between your black and white feelings evaporates, leaving you in a war with yourself that I cannot understand or help you with, though I try,
So that while you're sitting in the spaces where things used to make sense, you can't make sense, no matter how you try to rearrange the fragments of truth and whispers of lies, therefore I can no longer make sense.

I try to break off pieces of the black and white and crush them together to understand you, to create the colour that has consumed you, but it is only your colour to make, your colour to extract and turn it back into black and white.

While you are filled with everything you need to know and feel, I am left looking at the black lines on this white sheet, I know nothing but feel everything.

Mood swing

It's annoying the way my mood swings,
Back and forth like an excited child in the park, squealing to go higher,
and in that moment I hold my breath with my eyes closed counting from one to ten trying to get my ADHD of a mood swing to calm down, to slow down, to get off the swings, to leave the park.
But like a child, my mood doesn't know how to control itself when it's all fired up, it now charges forward and shouts "TO THE SEESAWS!" and I watch myself as if I have stepped out of my body, as my mood is high and I am ok, content, good, and as it quickly descends, I am sad, angry, indifferent.

My mood is also a budding gymnast as it tries to astound the crowd by walking carefree across a tight rope, tightly pulling on my thin rope, that could lead me to snap at someone any minute,
Proud of itself, it jumps off and like a child high on lollipops and sugar it runs around and around in circles, and I hold my head in despair, not quite knowing how to feel, getting angry when someone asks "what's wrong?" because I don't know, my emotions are in circles, running too quickly for me to stretch my hand out and grab just one.

How do I calm down a mood swing? Do I feed it chocolate and pizza? Do I try to make it go to sleep by sleeping myself? Do I send myself to my room and hibernate the whole day? It's hard to deal with a mood swing,
So then unfortunately it's going to be hard to deal with me today.

Star in the making

A Super nova is when a star has used up all of its hydrogen, it dies in a violent explosion which radiates as much energy as the sun.

They say humans are made up of that stardust, the atoms in our body were made in the furnace of those super nova's.

So to those who think they aren't special, just another person in this world, you were fearfully and wonderfully made, loved so much that stardust was put in your very being.

You may think that you are broken, existing only as a million pieces but you are magical like the fireworks that explode in the night sky, shooting out beautiful colours that leave the rest of the world in awe.

That when you sigh so deeply letting all that air escape you, it has already lived through it all before, telling stories older than you can imagine.

Blinded by the pain of life that desperately demands to be felt, you're unaware of the beauty that lies in and out of your very skin, that the atoms that danced around inside a shining light, now emits from your lips every time you smile.

So when you feel alone and your world is a little black, that's the best time to remember, that only stars shine in the dark.

The first time I saw tears in your eyes rise up high like an
incoming wave,
And choke on the words that were meant to come out but
slid down your tongue and got caught in your throat,
It was in that moment that I knew those tears were
messengers for me,
Describing the undistinguishable love you felt for me

Heaven but Hell

When you're filled with butterflies that flitter to only music you can hear,
As if they're in a magical, desirable world of their own,
Every cloud had a silver lining that shimmers so beautifully,
You smile for a thousand people as if you have a secret no one knows,
There was a part of you that was missing but you didn't realise until now,
You feel so whole you could explode and you treasure the fact no everyone feels it,
Your eyes are filled with a sparkle and your body gives off a glow,
You feel you have never been so happy,
You want to be with them every day and embrace their touch,
You feel you are so safe when they wrap their arms around you.
A whisper in your ear leaves an imprint on your childlike mind, and certain words leave an imprint on your heart,
It's considered the best feeling in the world,
But even the most wonderful feeling in the world can hurt the most,
It causes you inner stress and anxiety,
You could cry a thousand tears but it would never be enough,
You could cut yourself to hide the pain behind the scars but it would never work,
You could try and move on and forget,
But what's printed on your heart and mind lasts a lifetime.
It never gets easier every time it comes around,
But it only lasts as long as you let it,
So they say.
You could hurt so bad and so deep that nothing physical can take it away,

You feel like you've been killed but cannot die and no one understands you,
No one could possibly empathise as much as they try to.
The spark slowly fades from your eyes,
And the glow you once perceived is evilly snatched back,
The colours drain from the world around you and you want to be left alone...but at the same time you don't,
You want the pain to so badly go but it won't,
All you want is to feel how you felt before as it cannot be gained artificially,
You realise it's a gamble to see how long you can feel unstoppable,
And how long you won't feel destructible, it slowly continues to play back and forth.
People forever give their hearts,
Have it broken,
And slowly repair it for the cycle of never ending pain, suffering, happiness and desire to continue,
the cycle of true love

The grass isn't always greener on the other side

I guess you have to find that out in your own way,
There was me packing up and moving miles away thinking this was the key,
to inner happiness that I had lost on this bumpy road somewhere between the Cheshire Cat and something with more useful directions,
There was no more colour in my world, no more bounce in my step,
My smiles had turned to straight lines, my cheeks always wet.

So I picked up my things, climbed over the white picket fence and ran to dance on the grass on the other side

"The grass isn't always greener on the other side",
The wind whispered as it snatched my breath away and pushed me further in,
The grass that seemed to grow strong and sturdy were nothing but dead patches here and there,
I looked back to the other side of the fence...the grass seems just as green now...
wow...
Is all I could think,
I was so busy hiding from trouble and drama, the dynamic duo who wouldn't leave my side,
That I ended up wearing rose coloured glasses thinking anywhere was better than here...
But here is where I am,
Turns out it's the same grass, just a different location,
Nothing much has changed at all, same situations.

"The grass isn't always greener on the other side",
Trouble whispered to me with a Cheshire Cat grin,
As drama danced around me in circles, knocking over my
suitcase of freedom, spilling my cup of happiness and messing
up my bed of future adventures.

"The grass isn't always greener on the other side",
I said to myself as I sat under a tree with the leaving falling
gently beside me, turning a beautiful brown colour for autumn
(or fall),
Was I a fool for thinking running away would change my life?
Or that getting rid of sadness would fix my broken heart?

Maybe I'll climb back over the fence, back to the other side,
where people on this side must think is greener,
Maybe I'll even fertilise it while I'm there...

Sometimes it rains a little longer than it should

Sometimes it rains a little longer than it should,
Sometimes it hurts a little more than I wish it would,
Sometimes when I feel like I've reached rock bottom,
I'm still falling,
Sometimes when I think, maybe I should say something,
I'm still stalling,
Sometimes even when I have so many people in my life,
I can still feel so alone.

Sometimes it rains a little longer than it should,
The raindrops become bigger and heavier,
Where they used to be little trickles down my window,
The sound hardly noticeable,
They've now teamed up with hailstones,
Making what should be harmless drops of rain,
Into showers of never ending rain with a little bit of pain if you
come into contact with it or the sounds of something violent
trying to break your windows like it acts as a fist trying to get in.

Sometimes it rains a little longer than I wish it would,
The rain seems to find itself inside of you, messing with your
heart and brain,
Then finding its way out through your eyes,
When you think you're finally done, something sets off inside
of you and you start another waterfall wishing you would stop,
Hoping no one sees you.

Sometimes it just rains,
And rains,
And rains,
And your upset just pains,

And pains,
And...pains,
All you can do is push through the tunnel,
Until you see a shimmer of light,
A glance of happiness,
A feeling of hope.

People say things always work out in the end,
You just have to be patient and let things fall into place,
And yes, it can feel as if time is moving so slow just to spite you,
That God won't take away the feelings you want gone because he's ignoring you,
That no good can come from the rain that is forever overflowing in you and leaking out of your eyes.

But one day you'll see time seemed slow to help you heal before you left the lakes and rivers to dive back into the waterfalls,
One day you'll see God didn't ignore you, he just wanted you to become stronger,
One day you'll see those tears tried to help you feel better, they were washing away the mud from the inside,
But until then,
Sometimes it has to rain a little longer than it should.

Bra

The one thing I don't understand is the mysteries of a bra,
What is the point of wearing them, if they're just going to leave
a dark scar or red markings right under your boobs?
Yes I get they're meant to hold them up, but that's a bit of a
challenge when both boobs can be a different sized cup.

It's not all that bad, what can beat the feeling of retail therapy,
but is it just me or is it a little awkward when some guy named
Jeremy is serving at the till. (No it's not the fact that his name is
Jeremy, but the fact that I can go all shy because the person
who has to serve me is a guy!)
Still, I suck it up and make sure I don't make too much eye
contact when I put the pretty bra's down on the desk, I wonder
if they look at the size of your bra and then try to check out
your chest.

And why is it that something that has so little material is a serial
killer to my money, it becomes so intense trying to find the right
bra's because of how expensive they are.

I do like putting on a new bra and carrying on with my day,
it just gives you a top up boost of confidence, even if no one
can see it, especially when it's the perfect fit, be it a balcony,
plunge, t-shirt bra or non wired.

But seriously are they hard wired to reach a certain time in the
day to start getting on your nerves? The shoulder straps may
fall down, or your boobs are trying to escape or the strap at
the back starts to dig in, it's as if my body is screaming "I want
to be free like Adam and Eve!"
And then the main focus switches and the aim of the game is
to now get home and take it off and what a relief your whole

body feels when your boobs take flight...with gravity...I know it's not just me,

And then the red tribal markings left by the bra start to itch and you have to hitch up you boobs to really get a good scratch, no guy will truly understand that feeling of winning, no guy will truly understand that once that bra has come off, it is game over, there is no coming over or me coming out, my bra is across the room and that's where it will stay until tomorrow morning when I have to go out and deal with feeling all over again.

They say love hurts,
Love doesn't hurt, it's the pain that comes from heartache
that hurts,
It's the arguments and tears that hurt,
It's the growing apart that hurts.

They say love is blind,
Love isn't blind, Lust is blind,
Infatuation is blind,
Love sees everything, it sees what the eyes can't see,
It sees past what the eyes see.

Love will love you when you hurt,
Love will love you because you're not perfect,
Love will kiss your every imperfection and tear and tell you it
will get better.

14493646R00065

Printed in Great Britain
by Amazon.co.uk, Ltd.,
Marston Gate.